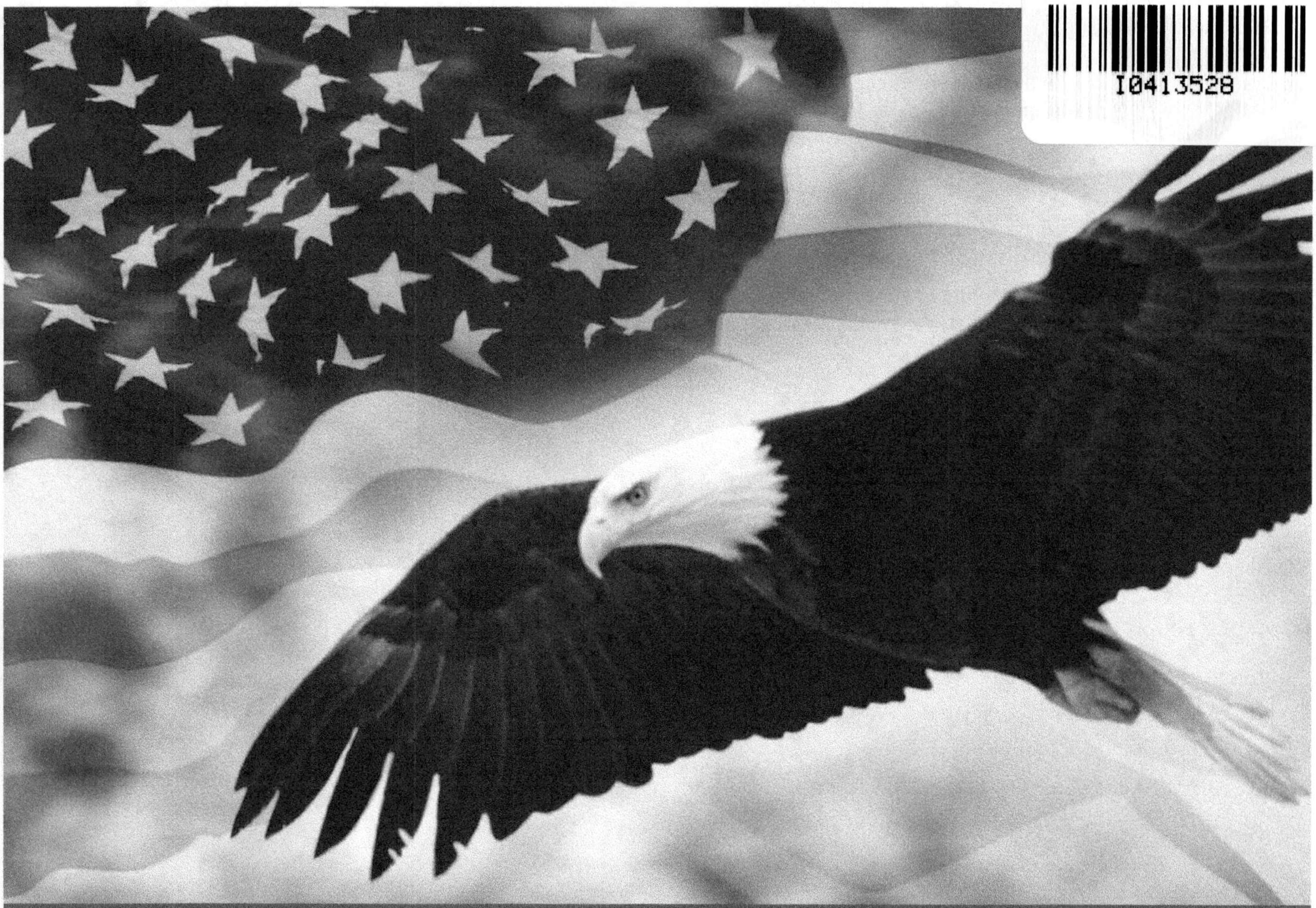

A Whole Community Approach to Emergency Management: Principles, Themes, and Pathways for Action

FDOC 104-008-1 / December 2011

Table of Contents

Introduction

The effects of natural and manmade disasters have become more frequent, far-reaching, and widespread. As a result, preserving the safety, security, and prosperity of all parts of our society is becoming more challenging. Our Nation's traditional approach to managing the risks associated with these disasters relies heavily on the government. However, today's changing reality is affecting all levels of government in their efforts to improve our Nation's resilience while grappling with the limitations of their capabilities.[1] Even in small- and medium-sized disasters, which the government is generally effective at managing, significant access and service gaps still exist. In large-scale disasters or catastrophes, government resources and capabilities can be overwhelmed.

The scale and severity of disasters are growing and will likely pose systemic threats.[2] Accelerating changes in demographic trends and technology are making the effects of disasters more complex to manage. One future trend affecting emergency needs is continued population shifts into vulnerable areas (e.g., hurricane-prone coastlines). The economic development that accompanies these shifts also intensifies the pressure on coastal floodplains, barrier islands, and the ecosystems that support food production, the tourism industry, and suburban housing growth. Other demographic changes will affect disaster

Figure 1: Joplin, Missouri, May 24, 2011—Homes were leveled with the force of 200 mph winds as an F5 tornado struck the city on May 22, 2011. This scene is representative of the growing impacts of disasters. Jace Anderson/FEMA

management activities, such as a growing population of people with disabilities living in communities instead of institutions, as well as people living with chronic conditions (e.g., obesity and asthma). Also, communities are facing a growing senior population due to the Baby Boom generation entering this demographic group. Consequently, changes in transportation systems and even housing styles may follow to accommodate the lifestyles of these residents. If immigration trends continue as predicted, cities and suburbs will be more diverse ethnically and linguistically. Employment trends, when combined with new technologies, will shift the ways in which local residents plan their home-to-work commuting patterns as well as their leisure time. All of these trends will affect the ways in which residents organize and identify with community-based associations and will influence how they prepare for and respond to emergencies.[3]

---

[1] Resilience refers to the ability to adapt to changing conditions and withstand and rapidly recover from disruption due to emergencies. White House, "Presidential Policy Directive 8 (PPD-8)," March 30, 2011.

[2] Intergovernmental Panel on Climate Change, "Special Report on Managing the Risks of Extreme Events and Disasters to Advance Climate Change Adaptation," November 2011.

[3] Strategic Foresight Initiative, "U.S. Demographic Shifts: Long-term Trends and Drivers and Their Implications for Emergency Management," May 2011.
Strategic Foresight Initiative, "Government Budgets: Long-term Trends and Drivers and Their Implications for Emergency Management," May 2011.

This document presents a foundation for increasing individual preparedness and engaging with members of the community as vital partners in enhancing the resiliency and security of our Nation through a Whole Community approach. It is intended to promote greater understanding of the approach and to provide a strategic framework to guide all members of the emergency management community as they determine how to integrate Whole Community concepts into their daily practices. This document is not intended to be all-encompassing or focused on any specific phase of emergency management or level of government, nor does it offer specific, prescriptive actions that require communities or emergency managers to adopt certain protocols. Rather, it provides an overview of core principles, key themes, and pathways for action that have been synthesized from a year-long national dialogue around practices already used in the field. While this is not a guide or a "how-to" document, it provides a starting point for those learning about the approach or looking for ways to expand existing practices and to begin more operational-based discussions on further implementation of Whole Community principles.

National Dialogue on a Whole Community Approach to Emergency Management

In a congressional testimony, the Administrator of the Federal Emergency Management Agency (FEMA), Craig Fugate, described today's reality as follows: "Government can and will continue to serve disaster survivors. However, we fully recognize that a government-centric approach to disaster management will not be enough to meet the challenges posed by a catastrophic incident. That is why we must fully engage our entire societal capacity...."[4] To that end, FEMA initiated a national dialogue on a Whole Community approach to emergency management, an approach that many communities have used for years with great success, and one which has been gathering strength in jurisdictions across the Nation.

The national dialogue was designed to foster collective learning from communities' experiences across the country. It occurred in various settings, such as organized conference sessions, research seminars, professional association meetings, practitioner gatherings, and official government meetings. The various settings created opportunities to listen to those who work in local neighborhoods, have survived disasters, and are actively engaged in community development. Participants in this dialogue included a broad range of emergency management partners, including representatives from the private and nonprofit sectors, academia, local residents, and government leaders. The conversations with the various stakeholders focused on how communities are motivated and engaged, how they understand risk, and what their experiences are with resilience following a disaster. In addition, international and historical resiliency efforts, such as FEMA's Project Impact, were explored to gather lessons learned and best practices.[5]

FEMA also brought together diverse members from across the country to comprise a core working group. The working group reviewed and validated emerging Whole Community principles and themes, gathered examples of the Whole Community approach from the field, and

---

[4] Administrator Craig Fugate, Federal Emergency Management Agency, before the United States House Transportation and Infrastructure Committee, Subcommittee on Economic Development, Public Buildings, and Emergency Management at the Rayburn House Office Building, March 30, 2011.

[5] FEMA introduced Project Impact in 1997 as a national initiative designed to challenge the country to undertake actions that protect families, businesses, and communities by reducing the effects of natural disasters. The efforts focused on creating active public-private partnerships to build disaster-resistant communities.

identified people, organizations, and communities with promising local experiences. They participated in various meetings and conferences and, in some cases, provided the examples included in this document.

In addition to the national dialogue, this document was created concurrently with a larger effort to build an integrated, layered, all-of-Nation approach to preparedness, as called for by Presidential Policy Directive (PPD-8): National Preparedness.[6] As such, the Whole Community approach is being incorporated into all PPD-8 deliverables, including the National Preparedness Goal, National Preparedness System description, National Planning Frameworks, and the campaign to build and sustain preparedness nationwide, as well as leverage the approach in their development.[7] In support of these efforts, FEMA seeks to spark exploration into community engagement strategies to promote further discussion on approaches that position local residents for leadership roles in planning, organizing, and sharing accountability for the success of local disaster management efforts, and which enhance our Nation's security and resilience.

Whole Community Defined

As a concept, Whole Community is a means by which residents, emergency management practitioners, organizational and community leaders, and government officials can collectively understand and assess the needs of their respective communities and determine the best ways to organize and strengthen their assets, capacities, and interests. By doing so, a more effective path to societal security and resilience is built. In a sense, Whole Community is a philosophical approach on how to think about conducting emergency management.

There are many different kinds of communities, including communities of place, interest, belief, and circumstance, which can exist both geographically and virtually (e.g., online forums). A Whole Community approach attempts to engage the full capacity of the private and nonprofit sectors, including businesses, faith-based and disability organizations, and the general public, in conjunction with the participation of local, tribal, state, territorial, and Federal governmental partners. This engagement means different things to different groups. In an all-hazards environment, individuals and institutions will make different decisions on how to prepare for and respond to threats and hazards; therefore, a community's level of preparedness will vary. The challenge for those engaged in emergency management is to understand how to work with the diversity of groups and organizations and the policies and practices that emerge from them in an effort to improve the ability of local residents to prevent, protect against, mitigate, respond to, and recover from any type of threat or hazard effectively.

> **Whole Community is a philosophical approach in how to conduct the business of emergency management.**
>
> **Benefits include:**
> - Shared understanding of community needs and capabilities
> - Greater empowerment and integration of resources from across the community
> - Stronger social infrastructure
> - Establishment of relationships that facilitate more effective prevention, protection, mitigation, response, and recovery activities
> - Increased individual and collective preparedness
> - Greater resiliency at both the community and national levels

---

[6] President Barack Obama, "Presidential Policy Directive 8 (PPD-8): National Preparedness," March 30, 2011.
[7] FEMA, "National Preparedness Goal," September 2011. (Formally released on October 7, 2011.)

The benefits of Whole Community include a more informed, shared understanding of community risks, needs, and capabilities; an increase in resources through the empowerment of community members; and, in the end, more resilient communities. A more sophisticated understanding of a community's needs and capabilities also leads to a more efficient use of existing resources regardless of the size of the incident or community constraints. In times of resource and economic constraints, the pooling of efforts and resources across the whole community is a way to compensate for budgetary pressures, not only for government agencies but also for many private and

Figure 2: Madison, Tennessee, May 29, 2010—Gary Lima, Tennessee Emergency Management Agency Community Relations Coordinator, leads Boy Scout troop #460 in a Memorial Day project to place flags on graves. The picture reflects emergency managers becoming involved in the day-to-day activities of community groups. David Fine/FEMA

nonprofit sector organizations. The task of cultivating and sustaining relationships to incorporate the whole community can be challenging; however, the investment yields many dividends. The process is as useful as the product. In building relationships and learning more about the complexity of a community, interdependencies that may be sources of hidden vulnerabilities are revealed. Steps taken to incorporate Whole Community concepts before an incident occurs will lighten the load during response and recovery efforts through the identification of partners with existing processes and resources who are available to be part of the emergency management team. The Whole Community approach produces more effective outcomes for all types and sizes of threats and hazards, thereby improving security and resiliency nationwide.

Whole Community Principles and Strategic Themes

Numerous factors contribute to the resilience of communities and effective emergency management outcomes. However, three principles that represent the foundation for establishing a Whole Community approach to emergency management emerged during the national dialogue.

Whole Community Principles:

- **Understand and meet the actual needs of the whole community.** Community engagement can lead to a deeper understanding of the unique and diverse needs of a population, including its demographics, values, norms, community structures, networks, and relationships. The more we know about our communities, the better we can understand their real-life safety and sustaining needs and their motivations to participate in emergency management-related activities prior to an event.

- **Engage and empower all parts of the community.** Engaging the whole community and empowering local action will better position stakeholders to plan for and meet the actual needs of a community and strengthen the local capacity to deal with the consequences of all threats and hazards. This requires all members of the community to be part of the emergency management team, which should include diverse community members, social and community service groups and institutions, faith-based and disability groups, academia, professional associations, and the private and nonprofit sectors, while including government agencies who may not traditionally have been directly involved in emergency management. When the community is engaged in an authentic dialogue, it becomes empowered to identify its needs and the existing resources that may be used to address them.

- **Strengthen what works well in communities on a daily basis.** A Whole Community approach to building community resilience requires finding ways to support and strengthen the institutions, assets, and networks that already work well in communities and are working to address issues that are important to community members on a daily basis. Existing structures and relationships that are present in the daily lives of individuals, families, businesses, and organizations before an incident occurs can be leveraged and empowered to act effectively during and after a disaster strikes.

In addition to the three Whole Community principles, six strategic themes were identified through research, discussions, and examples provided by emergency management practitioners. These themes speak to the ways the Whole Community approach can be effectively employed in emergency management and, as such, represent pathways for action to implement the principles.

Whole Community Strategic Themes:

- Understand community complexity.
- Recognize community capabilities and needs.
- Foster relationships with community leaders.
- Build and maintain partnerships.
- Empower local action.
- Leverage and strengthen social infrastructure, networks, and assets.

In the *Strategic Themes in Practice* section of this document, the Whole Community concept is explored through real-world examples that highlight the key principles and themes of the Whole Community approach. In order to provide an illustration of how the principles and themes can be applied, examples for each of the five mission areas—Prevention, Protection, Mitigation, Response, and Recovery (as outlined in the National Preparedness Goal)—are included. In addition, examples from other community development and public safety efforts have been included—most notably, community policing. While the focus and outcomes may differ, such efforts have proven effective in advancing public health and safety and offer a model for emergency management personnel to consider. The *Pathways for Action* section provides a list of reflective questions and ideas for emergency management practitioners to refer to when they are beginning to think about how to incorporate the Whole Community concepts into their security and resilience efforts.

As a field of practice, our collective understanding of how to effectively apply Whole Community as a concept to the daily business of emergency management will continue to evolve. It is hoped that this document will assist emergency managers, as members of their communities, in that evolution—prompting new actions and soliciting new ideas and strategies. FEMA is committed to continued engagement in ongoing discussions with its partners in the public, private, and nonprofit sectors to further develop and refine strategies to deliver more effective emergency management outcomes and enhance the security and resilience of our communities and our Nation.

Strategic Themes in Practice

The strategic themes presented in this section speak to the various ways the Whole Community approach can be effectively employed in emergency management and, as such, represent pathways for action by members of the emergency management community at all levels. These themes and pathways are explored through the presentation of real-world examples that highlight how Whole Community concepts are being applied in communities across the country.

Understand Community Complexity

Communities are unique, multi-dimensional, and complex. They are affected by many factors and interdependencies, including demographics, geography, access to resources, experience with government, crime, political activity, economic prosperity, and forms of social capital such as social networks, social cohesion between different groups, and institutions. Developing a better understanding of a community involves looking at its members to learn how social activity is organized on a normal basis (e.g., social patterns, community leaders, points of collective organization and action, and decision-making processes), which will reveal potential sources (e.g., individuals and organizations) of new collective action. A realistic understanding of the complexity of a community's daily life will help emergency managers determine how they can best collaborate with and support the community to meet its true needs.

Figure 3: New Orleans, Louisiana, September 5, 2008—A bilingual volunteer helps non-English speaking evacuees, guiding them in the right direction to board the correct buses to their parishes. Understanding the complexity of communities (e.g., non-English speakers) helps emergency management practitioners to meet the residents' needs. Jacinta Quesada/FEMA

Understanding the complexities of local communities helps with tailoring engagement strategies and shaping programs to meet various needs. Numerous examples that involve local initiatives to identify, map, and communicate with a wide range of local groups exist nationwide. For example, the Houston Department of Health and Human Services (HDHHS) has been actively identifying ways to better communicate and plan with linguistically isolated populations (LIP) and limited-English proficient (LEP) populations within the city. HDHHS is working with about 20 community organizations that serve and represent LIP/LEP communities, along with Interfaith Ministries for Greater Houston, four refugee resettlement agencies that work with these populations, and several apartment complexes in southwest Houston (where many refugee and some immigrant populations live), in an effort to develop trusted relationships and ways to provide current preparedness, response, and recovery information. Because of this outreach, significant unmet needs (e.g., transportation) for these specific populations have been identified. The City of Houston is using this information to fulfill unmet needs for these populations and continues to work with these community organizations and private sector partners to improve outreach materials, methods of communication, and preparedness programs.

The full diversity of communities is better understood when communication and engagement efforts move beyond easy, typical approaches to looking at the real needs and issues a community faces. In one California city, the police noticed a high level of violent crime in a particular neighborhood. In a typical policing model, the police would have assigned additional officers to patrol the neighborhood, approached the community to provide them with information about the criminal activity, and informed residents of what they might do to avoid being affected by the crime. However, as part of an operational shift, the police took a proactive approach by first engaging with the community to obtain information about the nature and frequency of the local crimes. At the initial meeting, the police learned from the local residents that a number of problems contributed to the unsafe conditions of the neighborhood—problems that police response alone could not correct. Cars speeding through the neighborhood; the presence of abandoned cars, couches, and other litter in front yards; rundown conditions of apartment buildings; few safe walkways for neighborhood children; and a lack of lighting on street corners all contributed to the crime situation.

> **Understand Community "DNA"**
>
> Learn how communities' social activity is organized and how needs are met under normal conditions.
>
> A better understanding of how segments of the community resolve issues and make decisions—both with and without government as a player—helps uncover ways to better meet the actual needs of the whole community in times of crisis.

At the next community meeting, the police brought together a number of government departments, including fire, public works, and the housing authority, to address the residents' concerns. Government representatives agreed to provide dumpsters for the litter and the residents agreed to fill them. The community agreed to tow the abandoned cars and identified street repaving as a high priority. Together, the community and city officials approached the apartment owners, who agreed to paint the exteriors of the buildings. The public works department fixed the street lighting. Building upon the cooperation and the demonstrated responsiveness to the community's needs, several residents provided the police with information that led to the arrests of several individuals involved in the area's drug-related activities. In a relatively short period of time, police worked with local residents to transform what had been perceived to be a narrow crime issue into a broad-based community revitalization effort. Crime decreased, residents became involved, and the neighborhood was significantly improved. Emergency management practitioners can take a similar approach by understanding the underlying and core community concerns in order to build relationships and identify opportunities to work together to develop solutions that meet everyone's needs.

Numerous approaches exist to identify and better understand the complexities of local populations, how they interact, what resources are available, and the gaps between needs and solutions. For example, community mapping is a way to identify community capabilities and needs by visually illustrating data to reveal patterns. Examples of patterns may take into account the location of critical infrastructure, demographics, reliance on public transportation, available assets and resources (e.g., warehouses that can be used as distribution centers), and businesses that can continue to supply food or water during and after emergencies. Understanding communities is a dynamic process as patterns may change. Emergency managers and local groups often use community mapping to gather empirical data on local patterns. Revealing patterns can help emergency managers to better engage communities and understand and meet the needs of individuals by illustrating the dynamics of populations, how they interact, and available resources.

One community mapping program that the Washington State Emergency Management Division developed ("Map Your Neighborhood") won FEMA's 2011 Challenge.gov award for addressing community preparedness. This program helps citizens identify the most important steps they need to take to secure their homes and neighborhoods following a disaster. In addition, it helps to identify the special skills and equipment that neighbors possess, the locations of natural gas and propane tanks, and a comprehensive contact list of neighbors who may need assistance, such as older residents, children, and people with disabilities and other access and functional needs.

Recognize Community Capabilities and Needs

Appreciating the actual capabilities and needs of a community is essential to supporting and enabling local actions. For example, in response to past disasters, meals ready-to-eat (MREs) have been used to feed survivors because these resources were readily available. However, for a large portion of the population, such as children, seniors, or individuals with dietary or health considerations, MREs are not a suitable food source for various reasons, as MREs tend to contain high levels of fat and sodium and low levels of fiber.

Figure 4: Fargo, North Dakota, March 23, 2009—Thousands of students and community members work together with the National Guard at the Fargo Dome to make sand bags during a 24-hour operation. Community members have the capabilities to help meet their own emergency needs. Michael Reiger/FEMA

A community's needs should be defined on the basis of what the community requires without being limited to what traditional emergency management capabilities can address. By engaging in open discussions, emergency management practitioners can begin to identify the actual needs of the community and the collective capabilities (private, public, and civic) that exist to address them, as the role of government and private and nonprofit sector organizations may vary for each community. The community should also be encouraged to define what it believes its needs and capabilities are in order to fully participate in planning and actions.

Based on a shared understanding of actual needs, the community can then collectively plan to find ways to address those needs. Following the devastating tornadoes in Alabama during the spring of 2011, various agencies, organizations, and volunteers united to locate recovery resources in the community and communicate information about those resources to the public. Two days after the tornadoes, they formed the Alabama Interagency Emergency Response Coordinating Committee. The committee

> **Recognize Community Capabilities and Broaden the Team**
>
> Recognize communities' private and civic capabilities, identify how they can contribute to improve pre- and post-event outcomes, and actively engage them in all aspects of the emergency management process.

was led by representatives from Independent Living Resources of Greater Birmingham, United Cerebral Palsy of Greater Birmingham, and the Alabama Governor's Office on Disability. The committee also included representatives from FEMA and the American Red Cross.

A daily conference call was attended by as many as 60 individuals representing agencies that serve individuals with disabilities and chronic illnesses. In addition, volunteers with disabilities continuously scanned broadcast media and printed and electronic newspapers and called agency contacts to obtain the latest information on resources for disaster recovery. For instance, volunteers placed calls to local hospitals and clinics, faith-based organizations, and organizations representing clinical professionals to request help with crisis counseling. Recovery resource information was compiled in an extensive database with entries grouped within the following categories: Red Cross, FEMA, emergency shelters/housing assistance, medication assistance, health care services, mental health support, food assistance, eyewear, communications, computers/Internet, hiring contractors for home repairs, insurance claims, legal aid, vital documents, older adult care, childcare, blood donations, animal shelter and services, and emergency preparation. The Disaster Recovery Resource Database was updated twice daily and information was disseminated in multiple formats (e.g., email attachment, website, hard copy, and telephone).

The committee used local media outlets, state agencies (e.g., health, education, rehabilitation, aging, and mental health), city and county governments, the United Way's 2-1-1 Information & Referral Search website, and nonprofit organizations to disseminate the database to community residents. Independent Living Resources of Greater Birmingham hosted a website with recovery resources presented by category. This collaboration greatly enhanced the delivery of services to individuals with disabilities, as well as older residents.

As a protection effort, some communities have developed self-assessment tools to evaluate how prepared they are for all threats and hazards. One example is a Community Resilience Index (CRI), which was developed by the Gulf of Mexico Alliance's Coastal Community Resilience Priority Issue Team, the Mississippi-Alabama Sea Grant Consortium, and the Louisiana Sea Grant College

> **Plan for the Real**
> Plan for what communities will really need should a severe event occur and not just for the existing resources on hand.

Program in collaboration with 18 communities along the Gulf Coast, from Texas to Florida. It is a self-assessment tool and provides communities with a method of determining if an acceptable level of functionality may be maintained after a disaster. The self-assessment tool can be used to evaluate the following areas to provide a preliminary assessment of a community's disaster resilience: critical infrastructure and facilities, transportation issues, community plans and agreements, mitigation measures, business plans, and social systems. Gaps are identified through this analysis. The CRI helps to identify weaknesses that a community may want to address prior to the next hazard event and stimulates discussion among emergency responders within a community, thus increasing its resilience to disasters. As a result of the initial implementation of the Community Resilience Index (CRI), additional grant funding is being provided by the National Oceanic and Atmospheric Administration (NOAA) Coastal Storms Program to continue to build capacity in the region so facilitators can assist communities in taking the next steps. Under this new grant, facilitators will continue their work by helping communities identify issues and needs in connection with becoming more resilient, create a shared community understanding of the potential extent of future losses, apply strategies to serve near- and long-term mitigation needs, and take the first steps toward adapting to a rise in sea level. This support will be in the form of follow-up training and/or technical assistance.

Foster Relationships with Community Leaders

Within every community, there are many different formal and informal leaders, such as community organizers, local council members and other government leaders, nonprofit or business leaders, volunteer or faith leaders, and long-term residents, all of whom have valuable knowledge and can provide a comprehensive understanding of the communities in which they live. These leaders can help identify activities in which the community is already interested and involved as people might be more receptive to preparedness campaigns and more likely to understand the relevancy of emergency management to their lives.

The Colorado Emergency Preparedness Partnership (CEPP) exemplifies the benefits of fostering relationships with community leaders. According to its website, "CEPP is a collaborative enterprise created by the Denver Police Foundation, Business Executives for National Security, and the Philanthropy Roundtable. It is a broad coalition to implement a voluntary, all-hazards partnership between business and government and, to date, is the product of many Colorado partners including leaders of the philanthropic community, Federal, state and local agencies, business, academia, and US Northern Command." CEPP has built these trusted relationships since its inception in 2008. When not responding to a disaster, Colorado Emergency Preparedness Partnership (CEPP) partners remain connected with their network through information bulletins and tap into their capabilities for smaller emergencies and other needs. For example, the police recently needed a helicopter for a murder investigation and they contacted CEPP, a trusted partner, to see if there was one available. Within 30 minutes, three helicopters were offered by three different member organizations.

As suggested previously, disaster-resilient communities are, first and foremost, communities that function and solve problems well under normal conditions. By matching existing capabilities to needs and working to strengthen these resources, communities are able to improve their disaster resiliency. Community leaders and partners can help emergency managers in identifying the changing needs and capabilities that exist in the community. Community leaders can also rally their members to join community emergency management efforts and to take personal preparedness measures for themselves and their families. The inclusion of community leaders in emergency management training opportunities is a way to reach individuals, as these leaders can pass preparedness information to their members. They can be a critical link between emergency managers and the individuals they represent. Many emergency management agencies, such as the New York City Office of Emergency Management, include their private sector partners in regular exercises, sustaining and strengthening their relationships in the process.

> **Meet People Where They Are**
>
> Engage communities through the relationships that exist in everyday settings and around issues that already have their attention and drive their interactions. Connect the social, economic, and political structures that make up daily life to emergency management programs.

For example, central Ohio is home to the country's second-largest Somali population. The Mid-Ohio Regional Planning Commission has been working to gather information about this group's preferred communication methods, traditions, behaviors, and customs in order to appropriately plan for its needs in the event of an emergency. The Somali population requested that planners include the Somali community leaders in emergency preparedness and response efforts because they were the foremost sources of trustworthy communication. Both emergency managers and the community benefit from developing these trusted relationships.

Trust is a recurring theme that underpins healthy and strong communities. It acts as the glue that holds different groups together, strengthens and sustains solidarity, and supports the means for collective action. It is crucial that partnerships are based on trust and not on fear or competition to ensure the success of the Whole Community approach. Building social trust requires more than conventional outreach focused on "trust issues"; it requires collaborating with communities in joint activities designed to address specific local problems. As emergency managers and community leaders work together to solve problems, trusted relationships are formed as they learn to support and rely on one another. Fostering relationships and collaborating with community leaders is a way to build trust within the broader community as they are the links to individual community members. To this end, it is important that the government and its partners are transparent about information sharing, planning processes, and capabilities to deal with all threats and hazards.

> **Build Trust through Participation**
>
> Successfully collaborating with community leaders to solve problems for non-emergency activities builds relationships and trust over time.
>
> As trust is built, community leaders can provide insight into the needs and capabilities of a community and help to ramp up interest about emergency management programs that support resiliency.

Build and Maintain Partnerships

While certainly not a new concept, building relationships with multi-organizational partnerships and coalitions is an exemplary organizing technique to ensure the involvement of a wide range of local community members. The collective effort brings greater capabilities to the initiatives and provides greater opportunities to reach agreement throughout the community and influence others to participate and support activities. The critical step in building these partnerships is to find the overlapping and shared interests around which groups and organizations are brought together. Equally important is to sustain the motivations and incentives to collaborate over a long period of time while improving resilience through

Figure 5: Tuscaloosa, Alabama, June 9, 2011—The Japanese International Cooperation Agency made a donation of several pallets of blankets to representatives from several faith-based and volunteer organizations. The donation came in the wake of the April tornados that hit the southeast. Tim Burkitt /FEMA

increased public-private partnership. As FEMA Administrator Craig Fugate stated at the first *National Conference on Building Resilience Through Public-Private Partnerships,* "We cannot separate out and segment one sector in isolation; the interdependencies are too great.... We want the private sector to be part of the team and we want to be in the situation where we work as a team and not compete with each other."[8]

---

[8] Administrator Craig Fugate, Federal Emergency Management Agency, First National Conference on Building Resilience through Public-Private Partnerships, August 2011.

Businesses play a key role in building resilient communities. As businesses consider what they need to do to survive a disaster or emergency, as outlined in their business continuity plans, it is equally important that they also consider what their customers will need in order to survive. Without customers and employees, businesses will fail. The ongoing involvement of businesses in preparedness activities paves the way to economic and social resiliency within their communities.

An example of a public-private partnership that successfully negotiated difficult community political and economic dynamics comes from Medina County, just southwest of Cleveland, Ohio. Like so many urban areas, expansion into rural areas placed new demands on water supplies. Some homebuilders initially wanted to develop large plots that would require filling in existing wetlands and natural floodplains. The building plans also required firefighting services to truck in large amounts of water in the event of an incident.

A broad-based coalition that included the local government, county floodplain manager, planning commission, homebuilders association, and emergency manager came together to spearhead a process to promote development in the county while protecting water supplies and preserving wetlands and ponds. The partnership achieved a building standard that allowed builders to develop their desired housing design but also required them to build ponds and wetlands within each housing subdivision in an effort to sustain water supplies and allow for improved fire protection and floodplain management. The zoning and land use mitigation efforts promoted and protected the health, safety, and welfare of the residents by making the community less susceptible to flood and fire damage.

Working as a public-private partnership enabled the participants to reach an agreement and institutionalize it through cooperative legal processes. Mutual interests and priorities brought this otherwise disparate group together to form a productive partnership.

Partners to Consider Engaging

- Community councils
- Volunteer organizations (e.g., local Voluntary Organizations Active in Disaster, Community Emergency Response Team programs, volunteer centers, State and County Animal Response Teams, etc.)
- Faith-based organizations
- Individual citizens
- Community leaders (e.g., representatives from specific segments of the community, including seniors, minority populations, and non-English speakers)
- Disability services
- School boards
- Higher education institutions
- Local Cooperative Extension System offices
- Animal control agencies and animal welfare organizations
- Surplus stores
- Hardware stores
- Big-box stores
- Small, local retailers
- Supply chain components, such as manufacturers, distributors, suppliers, and logistics providers
- Home care services
- Medical facilities
- Government agencies (all levels and disciplines)
- Embassies
- Local Planning Councils (e.g., Citizen Corps Councils, Local Emergency Planning Committees)
- Chambers of commerce
- Nonprofit organizations
- Advocacy groups
- Media outlets
- Airports
- Public transportation systems
- Utility providers
- And many others…

Partnerships are attractive when all parties benefit from the relationship. The State of Florida established a team dedicated to business and industry. This dedicated private sector team is composed of various state agencies/organizations and business support organizations. The purpose of this team is to coordinate with local, tribal, state, territorial, and Federal agencies to provide immediate and short-term assistance for the needs of business, industry, and economic stabilization, as well as long-term business recovery assistance. The private sector team's preparedness and response assistance may include accessing financial, workforce, technical, and community resources. Local jurisdictions in the state are also incorporating this concept into their planning processes. Such partnerships help get businesses back up and running quickly after a disaster so they can then assist with the response and recovery efforts.

> **Create Space at the Table**
>
> Open up the planning table and engage in the processes of negotiation, discussion, and decision making that govern local residents under normal conditions.
>
> Encourage community members to identify additional resources and capabilities. Promote broader community participation in planning and empower local action to facilitate buy-in.

Throughout 2011, the Miami-Dade County Department of Emergency Management, in partnership with Communities United Coalition of Churches, the American Red Cross--South Florida Region, FEMA, Islamic Schools of South Florida and many others, conducted a pilot effort to identify what works and what does not work in engaging the whole community in emergency preparedness, response, and recovery. The following seven target population groups were chosen: low-income and disadvantaged residents, seniors, immigrants and those with limited English-speaking abilities, those of minority faith traditions, disabled people, youth, and the homeless. Given the size, diversity (e.g., ethnicity, religion, and age), and breadth of experience of Miami-Dade County Emergency Management, many lessons could be learned by focusing Whole Community efforts on this geographic area. Most notably, the pilot identified previously unknown assets that the target population groups could bring to an emergency situation, which resulted in the following developments:

- A network of 25 newly affiliated groups now partnering with emergency management and the Red Cross;

- Identification of 65 houses of worship, community groups, and religious broadcasters who can support disaster communications and language translation;

- New capacity to serve 8,000 survivors;

- Nine facilities already in the community identified as potential new sites for feeding and sheltering; and

- Five existing facilities identified as new points of distribution for commodities.

Following the pilot and despite significant budget cuts, Miami-Dade emergency management officials established a team of people to work over the next two years to institutionalize Whole Community into the way the department thinks, plans, and acts.

Once partnerships have been established, relationships like the ones created in Miami-Dade can be sustained through regular activities. Community ownership of projects will help ensure continued involvement and progress in the future. Furthermore, engaging community members through routine resilience-building activities, such as business continuity-related exercises, will ensure they can be activated and sustained during emergencies.

Including partners such as representatives from for-profit and nonprofit private sector organizations and individuals from the community in preparedness activities (e.g., emergency management exercises) is a way to maintain momentum. One key aspect of maintaining partnerships is to set up regular means of communication with community groups and local leaders, such as through newsletters, meetings, or participating volunteers, to ensure that they stay informed about and engaged in emergency management activities. The Agua Caliente Band of Cahuilla Indians sends out a monthly outreach newsletter that includes emergency preparedness updates. Contact information is provided in the newsletter to encourage community members to provide feedback on emergency management programs. The tribe also uses social media applications like Twitter and Facebook to update the community on emergency management issues and programs.

Emergency managers can continue to build and maintain partnerships that emerge during the response phase, enabling a better response when another disaster strikes. For example, Support Alliance for Emergency Readiness Santa Rosa (SAFER) is a network of organizations committed to serving actively during disasters. It was developed to bring together local businesses and faith-based and nonprofit organizations to provide more efficient service to disaster survivors after Hurricane Ivan devastated northwest Florida. The network's coordinating efforts were aimed specifically at eliminating unnecessary duplication of effort.

During non-emergency periods, SAFER works closely with other agencies to address the needs of the county's impoverished and vulnerable populations. In connection with this, SAFER helps families who lose their homes to fire, replenishes local food pantries, and provides cold weather shelters to the homeless. The relationships it forms while serving community residents daily provides the foundation for collective action when disaster strikes.

Empower Local Action

Recognition that government at all levels cannot manage disasters alone means that communities need the opportunity to draw on their full potential to operate effectively. Empowering local action requires allowing members of the communities to lead—not follow—in identifying priorities, organizing support, implementing programs, and evaluating outcomes. The emergency manager promotes and coordinates, but does not direct, these conversations and efforts. Lasting impacts of long-term capacity building can be evident in an evolving set of civic practices and habits among leaders and the public that become embedded in the life of the community. In this regard, the issue of social capital becomes an important part of encouraging communities to own and lead their own resilience activities.[9] Furthermore, community ownership of projects provides a powerful incentive for sustaining action and involvement.

In May 2011, a devastating tornado struck Joplin, Missouri, leading to the development of the Citizens Advisory Recovery Team (CART). CART is composed of city officials, business leaders, community leaders, and residents whose shared purposes are to engage residents to determine their recovery vision and share that vision with the community; provide a systematic way to address recovery through a planning process; and bring all segments of the community

---

[9] "By analogy with notions of physical capital and human capital—tools and training that enhance individual productivity—'social capital' refers to features of social organization such as networks, norms, and social trust that facilitate coordination and cooperation for mutual benefit." Putnam, Robert D., "Bowling Alone: America's Declining Social Capital," Journal of Democracy 6:1, Jan 1995, 65-78, p. 67.

together to share information and work together.[10] Shortly after the tornado, CART, with support from FEMA's Long-Term Recovery Task Force, Housing and Urban Development, Environmental Protection Agency, and the American Institute of Architects, conducted extensive public input and community sessions to discuss: housing and neighborhoods, schools and community facilities, infrastructure and environment, and economic development. All of the ideas and comments from these meetings were used to draft a recovery vision as well as goals and project concepts. Recommendations were then presented to the City Council in November 2011.

Similarly, following the 2008 flood in Cedar Rapids, Iowa, the city came together to identify the capabilities of agencies and organizations that could assist with the recovery. Representatives from state, county, and city governments, the chamber of commerce, schools, businesses, faith-based organizations, nonprofit organizations, and neighborhood associations, many of which were involved in the response to the flood, formed the Recovery and Reinvestment Coordinating Team (RRCT). They explicitly forged the partnership to help create a framework for recovery that would include the broad interests of the entire area.

The RRCT organized open houses and general public meetings for hundreds of residents and business owners in an effort to develop a community-wide discussion on the priorities for long-term revitalization and investment in the city. They also focused the public discussions on the need to integrate the revitalization plan with a flood protection plan. Out of these efforts, the RRCT established the Neighborhood Planning Process to oversee the city's post-flood Reinvestment and Revitalization Plan. The Reinvestment and Revitalization Plan included area action plans, goals, timelines, and redevelopment strategies for all ten affected neighborhoods, ultimately turning the recovery effort into an opportunity for redesigning and revitalizing the city.

> **Let Public Participation Lead**
> Enable the public to lead, not follow, in identifying priorities, organizing support, implementing programs, and evaluating outcomes. Empower them to draw on their full potential in developing collective actions and solutions.

Strengthening the government's relationship with communities should be based on support and empowerment of local collective action, with open discussion of the roles and responsibilities of each party. This vision should be clearly conveyed so that participating organizations can commit adequate resources over the long term and have a clear understanding of what the desired outcomes will be. Engaging members of communities as partners in emergency planning is critical to developing collective actions and solutions.

Two consecutive tragedies involving youth in a city in Colorado caused community members to recognize a need to better educate their youth on emergencies. A local fire department battalion chief helped form a small group of volunteers from the fire and police departments, enlisted support from a local television station's meteorologist, and began offering clinics and classes. Other agencies joined the effort and the group also began offering a Youth Disaster Training program for teenagers, hoping to engage the younger population in a broader, more meaningful experience through which emergency management skills and knowledge could easily be learned. The organizers found that when the teen participants became involved, the program's learning

---

[10] Citizens Advisory Recovery Team. Listening to Joplin: Report of the Citizens Advisory Recovery Team, Nov. 2011.

objectives and training approach were transformed from what had initially been envisioned. The teens rejected the program's original logo and redesigned it to be more meaningful to their peers. The teens also pressed for a different type of instruction. They wanted to hear from people who had actually survived a disaster and learn what the experience was like and how the survivors and relatives of victims felt afterward.

The Youth Disaster Training program became such a success that requests to participate quickly outstripped the available and planned resources. Other organizations, including public school leaders, state agencies, and other organizations, joined in. The teenagers brought their parents, informed their friends, and participated in activities such as a career development session during which they met emergency managers from the health, fire, and police departments, as well as the National Oceanic and Atmospheric Administration (NOAA) and FEMA. As a result of the summer program, the teenagers became empowered to voice their needs and interests and design and implement the best ways to fulfill them.

Empowering local action is especially important in rural communities where there tends to be less infrastructure (e.g., telecommunications, public transportation, and health services) and where emergency managers are often part-time employees who are also responsible for areas outside of emergency management. Rural communities understand that the social capital found in local volunteer organizations and individuals is necessary for preparing for and responding to unique rural threats such as agroterrorism. The Agrosecurity Committee of the Extension Disaster Education Network (EDEN) has established the Strengthening Community Agrosecurity Planning (S-CAP) workshop series to address challenges concerning the protection of agriculture and the food supply. Workshop participants include a wide range of community representatives (e.g., local emergency management and public health personnel, first responders, veterinarians, producers/commodity representatives, and agribusinesses). They come together to address the issues relevant to their specific agricultural vulnerabilities. The workshops help guide local Extension personnel and other community partners in developing the agricultural component of their local emergency operations plan to help safeguard the community's agriculture, food, natural resources, and pets. The workshops empower communities to build on their capacity to handle agricultural incidents through improved networking and team building.

Leverage and Strengthen Social Infrastructure, Networks, and Assets

Leveraging and strengthening existing social infrastructure, networks, and assets means investing in the social, economic, and political structures that make up daily life and connecting them to emergency management programs. A community in general consists of an array of groups, institutions, associations, and networks that organize and control a wide variety of assets and structure social behaviors. Local communities have their own ways of organizing and managing this social infrastructure. Understanding how communities operate under normal conditions (i.e., before a disaster) is critical to both immediate response and long-term recovery after a disaster. Emergency managers can strengthen existing capabilities by participating in discussions and decision-making processes that govern local residents under normal conditions and aligning emergency management activities to support community partnerships and efforts. Emergency managers can engage with non-traditional partners within their communities to build upon these day-to-day functions and determine how they can be leveraged and empowered during a disaster.

Communities are extremely resourceful in using what is available—in terms of funding, physical materials, or human resources—to meet a range of day-to-day needs. Whether relying on

donations and volunteers to stock a local food bank or mobilizing neighbors to form "watch groups" to safeguard children playing in public parks, communities have a great capacity for dealing with everyday challenges. There are opportunities for government to support and strengthen these pathways, such as providing planning spaces where people can meet and connect, providing resources to support local activities, and creating new partnerships to expand shared resources. Enhancing the successful, everyday activities in communities will empower local populations to define and communicate their needs, mediate challenges and disagreements, and participate in local organizational decision making. As a result, a culture of shared responsibility and decision making emerges, linking communities and leaders in tackling problems of common concern.

Figure 6: Margaretville, New York, September 4, 2011—Volunteers came to help residents remove mud and salvage belongings from homes ruined by floodwaters on "Labor for Your Neighbor" weekend events following Hurricane Irene. Elissa Jun/FEMA

For example, the protection and resilience of the Nation's critical infrastructure is a shared responsibility involving all levels of government and critical infrastructure owners and operators. Prevention, protection, mitigation, response, and recovery efforts relating to the Nation's infrastructure are most effective when there is full participation of government and industry partners. The mission suffers (i.e., full benefits are not realized) without the robust participation of a wide array of partners.

Following September 11, 2001, communities discovered that partnerships with local rail enthusiasts can help strengthen the security of the Nation's rail network. Across the United States, thousands of rail enthusiasts, or "rail fans," enjoy a hobby that takes them to public spots alongside rail yards where they watch and photograph trains. Rail fans are drawn from across a community's social and demographic landscape. However, the heightened security measures that followed the terrorist attacks of September 11, 2001, resulted in law enforcement and rail security police becoming suspicious of rail fans photographing busy locations where commuter and freight trains clustered.

After two rail fans were detained by local police for taking pictures of trains, a public outcry arose from rail fans online and their national associations. Across the country, rail fans insisted that they were far from being a threat to security and were actually one of the rail network's best security assets because they were routinely in a position to observe suspicious behavior. A coalition of senior police officers, rail fans, and local elected leaders convened to review and resolve the conflict. The controversy subsided as police acknowledged the rights of rail fans to photograph trains from public locations and the rail fans publicly embraced the need for greater security around rail yards. Rail fans offered to help keep America's rail network safe from vandalism, terrorism, and other incidents by reporting situations that appeared to be out of the ordinary.

BNSF Railway, one of the largest freight rail companies in North America, developed a community-based rail fan reporting program called Citizens for Rail Security. This program includes a web-based reporting system in which rail fans can enter a minimal amount of their personal information, generate an official identification card, and receive guidelines on how to report any suspicious activities or potential security breaches.

Experiences in Haiti after the catastrophic earthquake in 2010 also underscore the value of leveraging existing social infrastructure. A research team that had worked for months after the disaster identified two different types of social and organizational networks providing aid to earthquake survivors.[11] One network consisted of large relief agencies that focused on transporting a large volume of humanitarian aid from outside the country and into the disaster area. The second type of network involved pre-existing social groups that routinely worked with and inside local Haitian neighborhoods to provide basic social services.

The network of large relief agencies had to create systems and gather manpower and equipment to distribute the aid, whereas the second group that used pre-existing social groups already had systems, manpower, and equipment in place. The unfamiliar network of large relief agencies was also plagued by aggression and theft by the locals, which the familiar pre-existing social groups did not experience. Since the network of pre-existing social groups routinely worked with and inside local Haitian neighborhoods to provide basic social services, they were trusted and had detailed knowledge of local conditions, which allowed them to anticipate local needs accurately and provide the aid required. Since they knew the actual amount of resources needed, they did not rely on large convoys that would be tempting to vandals.

Strengthen Social Infrastructure

Align emergency management activities to support the institutions, assets, and networks that people turn to in order to solve problems on a daily basis.

Many of the problems encountered in providing aid to Haiti resemble difficulties faced in other large-scale emergency response operations. Problems did not occur because of an absolute shortage of supplies or slow responses. Rather, they resulted from failures to connect with and benefit from the strengths of existing, familiar patterns of community interaction and assistance.

One reason why local community organizations are effective during emergencies is that they are rooted in a broad-based set of activities that address the core needs of a community. They are of, by, and with the community. They may be, for instance, involved in feeding and sheltering the homeless or working with children in after-school programs. They also remain visible in the community, communicating regularly with local residents about issues of immediate concern, as well as more distant emergency management interests.

---

[11] Holguín-Veras, José, Ph.D., et al., "Field Investigation on the Comparative Performance of Alternative Humanitarian Logistic Structures after the Port au Prince Earthquake: Preliminary Findings and Suggestions," March 2, 2011.

Pathways for Action

While there are many similarities that most communities share, communities are ultimately complex and unique. Ideas that work well in one community may not be feasible for another due to local regulations, available funding, demographics, geography, or community culture, for example. Some communities have fully integrated Whole Community concepts into their operations. For other communities, this is a new concept that they are hearing about for the first time. If this concept is familiar to you, think about what you can teach and share with others. On the other hand, if you are looking to begin a Whole Community approach or expand existing programs, the following questions and bullets may help get you started.

What follows are ideas and recommendations that were collected as part of the national dialogue during facilitated group discussions with emergency management practitioners from nonprofit organizations, academia, private sector organizations, and all levels of government. These recommendations are by no means exhaustive, but are intended to help you think about ways in which you can establish or broaden a Whole Community practice of emergency management within your community.

How can we better understand the actual needs of the communities we serve?

- Educate your emergency management staff on the diversity of the community and implement cultural competence interventions, such as establishing a relationship with a multi-lingual volunteer to help interact with the various groups.[12]

- Learn the demographics of your community. Develop strategies to reach community members and engage them in issues that are important to them.

- Know the languages and communication methods/traditions in the community—not only what languages people speak and understand, but how they actually exchange new information and which information sources they trust.

- Know where the real conversations and decisions are made. They are not always made at the council level, but at venues such as the community center, neighborhood block parties, social clubs, or places of worship. Tap into these opportunities to listen and learn more about the community. For example, homeowner association quarterly meetings (social or formal) may serve as opportunities to identify current community issues and concerns and to disseminate important public information.

What partnerships might we need in order to develop an understanding of the community's needs?

- Identify a broad base of stakeholders, including scout troops, sports clubs, home school organizations, and faith-based and disability communities to identify where relationships can be built and where information about the community's needs can be shared. Partner with groups that interact with a given population on a daily basis, such as first responders, places of worship, niche media outlets, and other community organizations. These

---

[12] For more information on cultural competence interventions, see Betancourt, J., et al., "Defining Cultural Competence: A Practical Framework for Addressing Racial/Ethnic Disparities in Health and Health Care," Public Health Reports, 2003, Vol. 118.

groups/organizations have already established trust within the community and can act as liaisons to open up communication channels.

- Every year, foreign-born residents and visitors are among those affected by disasters in our country. Reach out to local foreign country representatives through consulates or embassies to incorporate international partners in a Whole Community approach to domestic disasters.

How do we effectively engage the whole community in emergency management to include a wide breadth of community members?

- Reach out and interact with your Citizen Corps Council (or similar organization) to inquire about groups that are currently involved in emergency planning, as well as groups that are not involved but should be. Citizen Corps Councils facilitate partnerships among government and nongovernmental entities, including those not traditionally involved in emergency planning and preparedness. Additionally, Councils involve community members in order to increase coordination and collaboration between emergency management and key stakeholders while increasing the public's awareness of disasters.

- Strive to hire a diverse staff that is representative of the community.

- Maintain ongoing, clear, and consistent communication with all segments of the community by using vocabulary that is understood and known by those members.

- Discuss how organizations can have a formal role in the community's emergency plan and, when feasible, include them in training activities and exercises.

- Use the power of social media applications (e.g., Facebook and Twitter) to disseminate messages, create two-way information exchanges, and understand and follow up on communication that is already happening within the community.

- Involve children and youth through educational programs and activities centered on individual, family, and community preparedness.

- Develop recovery plans with full participation and partnership within the full fabric of the community.

- Incorporate emergency planning discussions into the existing format of community meetings. Multi-purpose meetings help increase participation, especially in communities where residents must travel long distances to attend such meetings.

- Identify barriers to participation in emergency management meetings (e.g., lack of childcare or access to transportation, and time of the meeting) and provide solutions where feasible (e.g., provide childcare, arrange for the meeting to be held in a location accessible by public transportation, and schedule for after-work hours).

- Consider physical, programmatic, and communication access needs of community members with disabilities when organizing community meetings.

How do we generate public interest in disaster preparedness to get a seat at the table with community organizations?

- Integrate the public and community institutions into the planning process by hosting town hall meetings and by participating in non-emergency management community meetings. Listen to the public's needs and discuss how individuals can play a role in the planning process.

- Make yourself available for local radio call-in programs to answer questions that callers have about emergency management and solicit input from the listeners on what they see as the top priorities for community resilience.

- Have an open house at your emergency operations center (EOC) and invite the public. Invite schools for field trips. Explain the equipment, organization, and coordination that are used to help protect the community.

How can we tap into what communities are interested in to engage in discussions about increasing resilience?

- Find local heroes and opinion leaders and learn what they are interested or involved in and tailor emergency management materials and information to meet their interests.

- Find out what issues or challenges various groups in your community are currently confronting, how they are organizing, and how emergency management might help them address pressing needs.

What activities can emergency managers change or create to help strengthen what already works well in communities?

- Understand how you can share and augment resources with partners within your community during emergencies. For example, providing a power generator to a store that has all the supplies the community needs but no power to stay open would be an example of a way in which to share and augment resources.

- Work with your partner organizations to better understand the various ways they will be able to prevent, protect against, mitigate, respond to, and recover from threats and hazards and supplement their activities and resources rather than compete with them.

- Identify organizations that already provide support to the community and determine how you can supplement their efforts during times of disaster when there might be a greater need. For example, if food banks distribute food on a regular basis, emergency managers can deliver additional food to the food banks to help them meet a greater demand during a disaster.

- Leverage existing programs, such as the local Parent Teacher Association (PTA), to strengthen emergency management skills in the community. Offer Community Emergency Response Team (CERT) training to PTA members.

How can communities and emergency management support each other?

- Provide adequate information to organizations ahead of time so they can better prevent, protect against, mitigate, respond to, and recover from threats and hazards. In return, organizations will provide you with information on their status and ability to assist when you need them. For this reason, ongoing multi-directional information sharing is one of the most important aspects of maintaining your partnerships. Have regular meetings with formal and informal community leaders and partners to maintain momentum.

- Provide support to for-profit private sector organizations in the development of business continuity plans. Keeping businesses up and running after an event helps to stabilize a community's economy and promotes resiliency.

When reflecting on the previous questions and ideas, it is important to remember that one size does not fit all. The definition of success will vary by community. Just as certain Whole Community efforts are appropriate for some communities and not for others, every jurisdiction has a different idea of what success means to them. Periodically assessing progress facilitates an ongoing dialogue and helps determine if the needs of the community are being met. Whole Community implementation requires flexibility and refinement through routine evaluation as lessons are learned. Communities should define metrics that are meaningful to them to track progress in the actions they choose to take toward meeting the communities' needs.

Regardless of what stage you are at in practicing Whole Community principles, think about how you can start or continue incorporating Whole Community principles and themes into what you do today. Test out your ideas and discuss them with your colleagues to learn and continue the national dialogue.

Conclusion

FEMA began its national dialogue with a proposition: A community-centric approach for emergency management that focuses on strengthening and leveraging what works well in communities on a daily basis offers a more effective path to building societal security and resilience. By focusing on core elements of successful, connected, and committed communities, emergency management can collectively achieve better outcomes in times of crisis, while enhancing the resilience of our communities and the Nation. The three core principles of Whole Community—understanding and meeting the actual needs of the whole community, engaging and empowering all parts of the community, and strengthening what works well in communities on a daily basis—provide a foundation for pursuing a Whole Community approach to emergency management through which security and resiliency can be attained.

Truly enhancing our Nation's resilience to all threats and hazards will require the emergency management community to transform the way the emergency management team thinks about, plans for, and responds to incidents in such a way to support community resilience. It takes all aspects of a community to effectively prevent, protect against, mitigate, respond to, and recover from threats and hazards. It is critical that individuals take responsibility for their own self-preparedness efforts and that the community members work together to develop the collective capacity needed to enhance their community's security and resilience.

Building community resilience in this manner requires emergency management practitioners to effectively engage with and holistically plan for the needs of the whole community. This includes but is not limited to accommodating people who speak languages other than English, those from diverse cultures or economic backgrounds, people of all ages (i.e., from children and youth to seniors), people with disabilities and other access and functional needs, and populations traditionally underrepresented in civic governance. At the same time, it is important to realign emergency management practices to support local needs and work to strengthen the institutions, assets, and networks that work well in communities on a daily basis.

To that end, FEMA will continue its national dialogue to exchange ideas, recommendations, and success stories. FEMA also intends to develop additional materials for emergency managers that will support the adoption of the Whole Community concept at the local level. As part of this ongoing dialogue, reactions and feedback to the Whole Community concept presented in this document can be sent to FEMA-Community-Engagement@fema.gov.

This document is just a start. It will take time to transform the way the Nation thinks about, prepares for, and responds to disasters. FEMA recognizes that the challenges faced by the communities it serves are constantly evolving; as an Agency, it will always need to adapt, often at a moment's notice. This shift in the Nation's approach to addressing the needs of survivors is vital in keeping people and communities safe and in preventing the loss of life and property from all threats and hazards. The Whole Community themes described in this document provide a starting point to help emergency managers, as members of their communities, address the challenge. However, it will require the commitment of members of the entire community—from government agencies to local residents—to continue learning together.